Telephone

poems by

Jen Besemer

Brooklyn Arts Press · New York

Telephone
© 2013 Jen Besemer

ISBN-13: 978-1-936767-23-6

Cover art by Jen Besemer. Design by Joe Pan.

Published in The United States of America by:
Brooklyn Arts Press
154 N 9th St #1
Brooklyn, NY 11249
www.BrooklynArtsPress.com
info@brooklynartspress.com

Distributed to the trade by Small Press Distribution / SPD
www.spdbooks.org

Library of Congress Cataloging-in-Publication Data

Besemer, Jen.
[Poems. Selections]
Telephone : poems / by Jen Besemer.
    pages cm
"Distributed to the trade by Small Press Distribution / SPD"--T.p. verso.
ISBN 978-1-936767-23-6 (Paperback : alk. paper)
I. Title.

PS3602.E775T45 2013
811'.6--dc23
                                        2013004201
FIRST EDITION

Acknowledgements

Special thanks to j/j hastain, my dear friend and collaborator, with whom I shared the poetic call-and-response practice adapted in *Telephone* for single-poet use. Many additional thanks to Max, Laura, Carol, and Nicholas (and j/j again) for conversing with this book, and for conversing with me about this book.

CONTENTS

phone   Tele-

dialogue one:
call

stone grows plump : its arms & laces under the earth
: stone erupts in compact pregnancies of tourmaline :
circumstances unforeseen : sharp ranges cut through
by threads of butter : the taken & the taker : each
quick to claim its own before : its own after ::

why must we chase our cool : the fear that drives the horse around the post drives the heart into a corner : false teeth grinning through the soul-stuff : look at how we chatter away & waste ourselves for weeks : rough tortoises nodding with our tongues in the wind : better make it good : the whole world is watching ::

some cup : full of word pebble : tiny lemon fort :
dream of conger in a crevice : ceviche saddle : make
a float & put a line on it : fend along the shore & pole
up pesce ::

ice that speaks : vast understatement of winter : forces
slide between weak & strong : free & taxed : naked
sun-birthed line between solid & vapor : note our
shadows : ink-blue & antennaed : a border flapping as
we walk : snow mouthing our shoes ::

make a heart with your hands : your knuckles & their
silent daybreak : mop up your only egg broken on the
tread : ascend & descend : baby buggy balance beam
: before the wilderness engulfs the kick ::

the bulge in my trousers is that blip in spacetime : my forests of magic christians & trees full of puppeteers : everybody loves a schism : treble peppers bass & makes trenchant song : mama gets her bullies in a row : pins the collars down for ironing : i have to rewind : i have to find my wormhole ::

dialogue one:
response

another nibelungenlied over the phone & the broken
mirrors clouding with a touch : fierce sentiment rises,
foam in a bottle, if the neck is long : the voice of ore
& root : what sort of argument is there today : forge
& mine are places & actions & quanta of association :
ghosts of animals rise with each fallen word : a name
like a sneer tearing at the earth we rest upon ::

a hand grips another hand : an eye watches both :
nostrils dilate : shallow breath edges inside : it seems
the skull echoes : somewhere a door has slammed : a
vibration of empty data : the message of the moment
shifts : one sees a flash like the feather of light just
before sunrise : one sees an injury as a burnt forest :
one sees time & how it departs ::

relocate to another dictionary & with that bucket
dredge up thick silence from the margins : a paste of
pages spread upon the brow : wrap my head in soft
candy flavored by essence of inquiry : sick with talk,
reach into the tongue : turn it inside out : dust it with
bone-slivers : begin again ::

the black box has a name : choose it from this list : write your choice in blue or black ink on the card provided : fold the card in half after you are done : be sure your choice is concealed from casual view : your privacy is important : leave the folded card in the upper right corner of your desk for collection : do not make eye contact with the proctor : your privacy is important : the black box has a name : your participation in this survey is much appreciated : it is entirely your choice : choose your benefit premium from this list : write your choice in blue or black ink on the card provided : fold the card in half after you are done : your privacy is important : do not make eye contact with the black box : the black box is important : it has a name : it is entirely your choice ::

children & elders walk single file down the canyon
path : in each pair of hands a fat candle the color of
yewberry : a hum of purposeful movement : the click
of teeth & garnet rings : the toss of a doll into a hole
in the earth ::

the moth gives up its dream of taming light : it loves
its life of silent paper & cool leaf-hair : it loves its
thinking tongue : its miles of wind : the doors of color
it sits beneath : the moth is only ever itself : the light
is light's own business : they are not our story ::

dialogue two: call

i'm so sick of this blue haze that spins from my mouth
whenever i speak : i can't turn my back anymore :
janus-faced, i can't help seeing : my horsemen are
always there : do we find each other in shadows or
in sun ::

people often confuse cause with effect : say that the
stone fell to the ground because it was found on the
ground : that the wall was built to hold the paint on
it : or the wildflowers edging the highway were put
there by cars : take the porpoise born to be fed fish
by a corporate swimmer in a neoprene uniform :
the sediment of error drifting like rotifers in water :
multiplying ::

wake, you sleepers : mate your shoes & place your
dreams three abreast upon your shelf : fill the basin &
dunk your belly : some trembling book expects your
fingers : some dark passage : the teasel in the meadow
shakes with laughter : *come, you cousin* : *wave your
wolf about & join us* ::

at one time there were names for the seven dances of deception : we forget them now : no one wants to learn how our elders were misled : no grants are given to researchers seeking evidence : no traces of choreographic notation for students wishing to see the folly of history : no fragile costumes : once or twice an inspired leap erupts & in fear of plagiarism all turn away : lower the eyes in desire or shame ::

the sport of vampirism requires expensive equipment but a good player never purchases gear : rely on the comfort of habitual behavior : a slick knife for licking : learn to mistrust other men's fingers : the ducks flocking to the iron shore : feel your memory become a series of seismic events : porous earth mixing with its opposite : it's all about the sun & the angle of descent ::

we recognize you by your anthracite lozenges : your desperate stain : the tiny crank that winds your tongue : you hold a flickering gaslight cradled in your arms like a steel lamb : we know you : we know the song you sing on rainy days : we follow you down alleys & watch you lay your forehead against the corners of brick buildings : we sit beside you in semi-legal diners, spooning dark soup into our analyzers : please come with us, now : come home, come home with us ::

dialogue two:
response

who walks alongside tight to your hip as though in a
three-legged race : who has your coins in his pocket
making a carnival sound : summoning children from
behind their bay windows & vinyl siding : whose fat
padlock bends your wrist : make a decision : there is
a word only you can write : open your hand ::

make a tent of your hands : put your eyes in there
: look out from the shelter of making : clear sight
despite rain ::

all the strangers are in their box now : their fool is
sleeping with his head in his coat : tomorrow's dance
is canceled & the road stretches out from the morning
: put no trust in jewels or peaches : the axle of the
wagon is all that matters : today is for moving forward
::

the sigh of the screen door like a council of widows
all wishing on their thumbs : the rust on the tank
next to the house : patient : rust & lichen tasting each
surface : the burden of living in time : as though it
were a gust of wind : the door opens, gasping : what
comes through ::

make a hole in the ground for the root ball : make a
hole in the stone for the cord : make a hole in the table
for the cup : make a hole in the window for the bird
: make a hole in the blanket for your mouth : make
a hole in the water for the fish : make a hole in the
canoe for the buttocks : make a hole in the wall for the
hand : make a hole in the soup for more soup : make a
hole in the pot for the stone : make a hole in the knife
for the hunter ::

run inside the thunder & hide : it is time for the known
world to fall to its knees : to make room for other
worlds & other knowings : time for this great flower
to dawn & stretch : time for thought to show its belly
: a sun is waiting : an ocean : we are the inventors of
time : a machine we do not know how to maintain :
we are young & quick to abreact ::

dialogue three:
call

make a ship of your hands : the long gaze of the sky :
your sails in the rings : bloom of salt at your wrists :
lick the waves onto your skin : travel new ::

an exile into sincerity is your doom : rabbits in a hedge
are no less hunted for their honesty : the trail will not
end here : the trail will never fade : each day the spoor
& tracks of a new trouble : what is the freedom that
must ask its own name with the rise of every sun ::

in a castle made of dust : particulate standards flapping : its moat of motes : the prince of nine sentences : his failures set in gold & made into a paw-shaped charm : the night sky pours black rope through the windows : bad advice greases the steps : each courtier mates with a crumbling cork effigy : spiders move the dungeon from place to place when no one's looking : no one ever looks : the unbearable silence & the smell of old bone ::

the road is littered with ripe lotus : scrotum-blush &
plump as pain : a theatre of ventures & advances :
fueled by bloom : after bloom : a touch wakes the
traveler : this is where we belong ::

we are waiting for a good idea : with our strollers circling the encampment we are waiting for a good idea : with the drums of our privilege in our hands we are waiting for a good idea : with the expectation of your agreement we are waiting for a good idea : with moss on our kneecaps we are waiting for a good idea : with our sharp eyes on your behavior we are waiting for a good idea : with our movement classes we are waiting for a good idea : with our teeth growing longer & more hollow we are waiting for a good idea : with our hands knotting our hair together we are waiting for a good idea : we are waiting for you to come a little closer ::

in the body there is another room : a carpet rolled out to welcome the deep-feeling ambassador : the fact-finders wait outside : who can tell them what to expect : your committee is still sequestered : you breathe slowly & it feels good : the room glows : the fact-finders are good-natured & serene : everything seems to be going well : your internal intern smiles : *yes i'd like a snack* : *yes with coffee* : & the door opens ::

dialogue three:
response

nails of phosphor : patent remedies : a book of
willingness to be read on the shore : treasure among
the shipwrecks : each gull wrestling with its seawrack
: each wave cresting with the potential to break into
pattern ::

the larger of the two questions : a cuckoo whose
mouth pulls in the sky : devouring the clouds : do you
hear the wind howl in the nest : do you hear the cry
: to survive this creature makes itself into an endless
belly : demands all things for its bread ::

fables & star-charts : which of these 360 steps shall
be the winning one : there are numerous wings to oil
: we need to get started : spin the arrow : land in the
space between : star-charts : the consultation craft :
the din of engines : what is necessary : what is most
necessary : move from square to square or degree to
degree : rough & miserly movements : force a wonder
by refusing to expect : a choice will demand itself ::

& in the spirit of the north we declare our intent : & in the face of the question we declare our intent : & in the path of the light we declare our intent : & in the doubt of our steps we declare our intent : & in the scent of roasted corn we declare our intent : & in the confines of the fishmarket we declare our intent : & in the belief of the sky we declare our intent : & in the name of the now we declare our intent : & in the shoals of our voices we declare our intent : & in the mud of the present we declare our intent : in the intent of our declaration we declare our intent to intend ::

the epiphytic dream : we stroke ourselves into being :
shadows cast in sphagnum & mold : to place each foot
on soft ground : to turn toward the motion of insects :
to wait with outstretched hand : we begin & end quietly
: & in surprise ::

the door is not a simple proposition : the diffuse
transaction : all at once moving from one instinct
to another : one knowledge to the next : to want to
pass through is understandable : to want to pass at
all anywhere : to want to stand on the threshold : to
lean shoulder braced against the bolted : to core the
understandable lock ::

dialogue four:
call

a brick wrapped in string : crisscross algorithm :
umbilical associations : a gestation as sabotage :
gestation *of* sabotage : do billionaires grow wings :
do wings mean what they once did : open your hands
: place them on the windowpane left & right : trace
them left & right : so you know where to aim later ::

a lion's forced intimacy with its prey : the great jaw
making much of the occasion : a ripple of tension in
the sleek pelt : one paw in the belly-wound : *gaucherie*
of the veldt : elbows on the table : observers note the
expression on the lion's face as it eats : like a clock in
a police station lobby : indiscreet ::

this time when the music starts the sorcerer's apprentice will do nothing : will remain absolutely still : will ignore his text message alerts & his software updates & the slightly disturbing crackle when he swallows : this time there will be no terrible accidents : nothing to clean up or put right : no workplace injuries or reports of unsafe conditions : no unpaid overtime & hostile environment : this time when the music starts the sorcerer's apprentice will sit down on the floor & rest his hands on his knees, just so ::

the color of new leaves becomes the basis for all our actions : the strength of the wind becomes the boundary of all our efforts : the sound of sleeping animals becomes the inspiration for all our ideas : the weight of the soil becomes the origin of all vantage points : the flavor of dust becomes the scale by which all light is measured : the sensation of the throat opening becomes the impetus for all motion ::

realization of sourness & fortitude : locks of hair tied
with string & pinned to the windowsill : wasp buzzing
its head against glass : lemonade in a tumbler on the
floor : destiny is a parrot on a tray : tongue like a beast
in its own right ::

there in the gutter of yesterday : a spring half crushed
with rust : motion & potential : we want to make
progress : we have a finger & a seal : a wish to board
a train & be given our trajectory : the oil of certainty
in our teeth ::

dialogue four:
response

the light under the bridge : a world : a terrace onto
empty being : grey stones of absence click in the hand
: sorrow toothy in the gut : stories of lack & haze :
overlapping through time : breathed in : webbing the
air ::

describe the passionless cruelty of ants : use these
words in your description : *mordant* : *guile* : *parquet*
: *bastion* : *gnarl* : *secant* : *dudgeon* : *tench* : *pump*
: *gillyflower* : *stun* : *fossil* : ask your dreams for
feedback : place your work in the correct envelope :
make sure you use the correct address : please provide
the correct postage ::

to find wilderness in the scraps of cloth held in fraying fingers : scarecrow-smiles in parcels of toys : bird cries in sand hissing fast & soft into a pail : an open mouth from which pours light like a thousand greyhounds : territories without maps : borders to be crossed & kissed : to find whole cities in the erasures of a manuscript of interrogations : rough magic of thwarted desire : denial : with pain ::

these bottles are full of moss : are our senators : are steps in a complicated procedure we have failed to learn : are days we have forgotten : are promises : are betrayals by trusted caregivers : are candies on a shelf : are desperate criminals on the run : these letters are new sponges meant to absorb time : are lives : are dishes from which the abandoned sup : are elements that combine to form a structure capable of supporting life : are breath ::

we take a dare with the strongest urge : the deepest
wish & the tallest dream : the sweetest cake on the
biggest plate : step & shake : dance with the nets of a
wild gift : answer the call inlaid in terrier teeth : front
to back : a wish ::

a blood of stars & serrated light : hydrogen & helium :
wake in the dark & stretch : feel the scurrying energies
: the food in the astonished void : stretch : your non-
hand tingling : the near-sound almost palpable : break
your fast with laughter & begin ::

dialogue five:
call

regime change : make a notion over in the image of a nation : make castles with material from continents away : make wi-fi & pizza puffs & instant noodles : what is human : an ancient reed basket made valueless ::

wire-limbed personages dance in numbered lines :
whiskers of thought radiate from faces made impudent
by translation : surrounded by forests of text the beat
of data quickens : the mother of motion is in me : the
doll with the wooden heart has vanished in song : the
cry of tomorrow advancing ::

valley-belly of smoke : fabric-encircled missiles with shark-fins & claw-feet : the soldiers have all eaten & are now at rest : the night awaits its orders & listens to its own coded breath : in sudden glee all hands open : their palms shine with the stars : they pull their brothers to them ::

meat : meat on a plate : meat on a plate with a block of salt : meat on a plate with a block of salt & a hammer : meat on a plate with a block of salt & a hammer made of emerald : meat on a plate with a block of salt & a hammer made of emerald on a table : meat on a plate with a block of salt & a hammer made of emerald on a table shaped like a boat : meat on a plate with a block of salt & a hammer made of emerald on a table shaped like a boat in drydock ::

these two senses have historically opposed one another : their respective teams kitted out in clashing colors : their contests quite as bloody now as they were millennia ago : their agitators are well paid to keep the antipathy fresh : whole cities sacrifice their self-esteem to the outcome of their combat : the fates of nations rest with the factions allied to one sense or the other : to compete is supreme : to defeat is godlike ::

a hollow moon alights on the tongue : hopping : slight
heat burst in froth of flavor : air swirls from between
the lips : the beginning of a cloud mass : a reminder
for a weather system : a down payment for spring ::

dialogue five:
response

my druidic forefathers suggest a holiday : broken out of the carapace of knowing & doing : a treat well-earned : my efforts rewarded by ripple of starlight : a row of new trees : my druidic forefathers approve heartily : their smiles become owls in the branches : their thumbs-up knuckling from the loam as mushrooms : dark & sweet ::

lodestone & birch bark : a strip of dried fruit on a slick yellow leaf : diamond air dappled with frost : the tears of the season : no easy phrase to reset the clocks by : no starting point marked on our board : these paths have met in a clearing without exit : no map : no guide but sleep ::

a knight swims in the channel : her helmet is the shell of a horseshoe crab : she holds somehow the standard of her army : it resembles a wheel : a sunfish : a lance of narwhal tusk is strapped to her back : her eyes flash with phosphor : she swims with a darting motion : i do not know her : curls of seaweed flow down her back : these marks on my hand are from her teeth : they spell a name ::

ochre powder slapped on walls : blown with reeds as though beast were tune : the aurochs & their dance delivered to the darkness : the aurochs are their own light : these wands of invocation are not ours : we take them up at our own risk : & know the song of the fear-blood in our ears ::

name that echoes in the head of the street cleaner : the
burn victim : the top chef : the newlywed : the game
show host : the card sharp : the heart surgeon : the
supermarket cashier : the architect : name that flavors
the tongue of the sportscaster : the metallurgist : the
diamond baron : the psychopath : the toddler : the
maid : it is *i* : it is *i* : it is *i* ::

some people are waiting outside in the lobby &
would like you to escort them : some people have a
lack of foreknowledge & want a hint : some people
discuss others' problems with a great deal of interest
& would like you to confide in them : some people
enjoy feeling the wind on the bare scalp & need a
breeze : some can't tell red from green & are fond of
that particular grey : some have such clear ideas & are
nowhere to be found ::

dialogue six:
call

the red velvet tongue of sleep : an understanding
reached between twilights : there are unknown
discussions without which nothing happens : a solid
secret wall : the mystery of day : the clouds that
determine the paths of light : what dreams the star
that dreams the language that shapes the mind ::

here is a shovel : it has a new handle : you can use it
to get your bearings : you can use it as a sundial : you
can use it as a sled : you can toss it up in the air &
head off in the direction it points when it lands : you
can use it to dig yourself an underground clubhouse :
you can decide to settle right where you are & plant
seeds for tomorrow : you'll need something that turns
the earth : so to speak ::

we know you : the sepia glow of the past is our doing
: we change those who see us on our paths : we speak
with arms : the idea of dance was ours : the thoughts
that whisper in your beds are ours : we have taught
the body how to dream apart from the mind : we
are the colors of your knowledge & the ink of your
yearning ::

this is a darkness : this is a nail : this is a pistol : this is a tree : this is a doubt : this is a story : this is a photograph : this is a snail : this is a colony : this is an injury : this is a policy : this is a source : this is a waterway : this is a beast : this is an artifact : this is a will : this is a table : this is a door : this is a cycle : this is a test : this is a life : this is a poem ::

make a forest with your hands : do you want the wolf
: do you want the woodcutter : the ancient little girl :
make a story out of blood : make the trees into teeth :
fear that blows in the leaves & makes them scraps of
flesh : children who flee in terror of their own bodies
: children forced into iron dresses & lead slippers : to
grow up half dead with worry over shapes & sizes &
the presence or absence that will never fully define
us ::

the act of walking into a place : the occupation of
being in space : existence as a body : action & reaction
in the newtonian sense : the molecular mesh : how
we become what we inhabit : how our surroundings
become us : the moving negotiation of *taking place* :
the breakdown of language for embodiment : there is
only ever energy : there is the habit of a body : only
habit ::

dialogue six:
response

the strange leap from before to after : a slice of
indeterminacy : the trick is not to see it as a blemish
: there are battalions of stylists waiting to conceal
the gap : be proud of the now you carry : you have
nothing to fear from nothing ::

does this tune create a sort of resonance between
self & other : can the process be condensed into a
repeatable description : the forms of knowledge at
our disposal are not always clear : the machines &
procedures not accessible : what part must we play in
our own contentment : what are the costs of failure ::

on the shore there is a path into the dunes : rise from
the sea & walk inland : a glimpse of strange potential
friends : a question working silently beneath the earth
: these pull you forward : these put your limbs on the
land : the basket of your jaw changing as the mirrors
fall from your flanks ::

a box has eight corners : you can't fool me : it has a
door & three windows : it has a motor for climbing &
racing : it has a ledge to place your hands on : out of
the way : it has a sort of vibration that helps it locate
its prey : it has a particular scent : half coffee & half
pineapple : it can learn to recognize its own name : it
can defend itself & its owner if properly trained : it
costs more than an elephant & eats everything it can
get its hands on ::

in the context of the commercial the handmade is
problematic : at once honored & devalued it becomes
a fiction : a fetish like the mother or the well-rounded
individual : the ideal is supported : is demanded :
while the actual is abandoned : this then is the task
of the hand : to make of itself itself & allow its user
to follow ::

our signal is not what it was : lost power, data-struggle : we are the broken talk of meat : a mass of lines with the words cut loose : stuck in a fat round closet echoing with interruption : clasp hands : after all it's still spring ::

JEN BESEMER is a hybrid artist and the author of four poetry chapbooks, the most recent being *Object with Man's Face* (Rain Taxi Ohm Editions). She is currently pursuing solo and collaborative projects in recombinant poetry, translation, performance, criticism, visual art, and combinations thereof. Recent work has appeared in *Artifice*, *Aufgabe*, *BlazeVOX*, *Drunkenboat*, *e-ratio*, *Otoliths*, and *Pank*, and is anthologized in *Troubling the Line: Trans and Genderqueer Poetry and Poetics* (Nightboat). Jen writes features and reviews for *Rain Taxi Review of Books* and teaches art and poetry workshops in and around Chicago. To learn more, visit www.jenbesemer.com.

Made in the USA
Charleston, SC
23 July 2013